Frances McNaughton's sugarcraft books have become international bestsellers. She has been a tutor and demonstrator for many years, teaching all aspects of sugarcraft to students from beginner to advanced level, and to other sugarcraft tutors. She travels all over Europe providing demonstrations and workshops for exhibitions, shops, groups and clubs, and has many fans in the US, Australia and New Zealand through her online tutorials and sugarcraft products. Frances made sugarcraft props for the films *Notting Hill, Chocolat, Charlie and the Chocolate Factory* and three of the *Harry Potter* films.

Sweet & Easy
Sugar Decorations

First published in Great Britain 2012

Search Press Limited
Wellwood, North Farm Road,
Tunbridge Wells, Kent TN2 3DR
Text copyright © Frances McNaughton 2012

Based on the following books published by Search Press:
Twenty to Make: Sugar Birds by Frances McNaughton (2011)
Twenty to Make: Sugar Animals by Frances McNaughton (2009)
Twenty to Make: Sugar Fairies by Frances McNaughton (2010)

Photographs by Debbie Patterson at Search Press Studios

Photographs and design copyright © Search Press Ltd 2012

ISBN: 978-1-84448-752-3

Suppliers
If you have difficulty in obtaining any of the materials and equipment mentioned
in this book, then please visit the Search Press website for details of suppliers:
www.searchpress.com

Printed in China

Sweet & Easy
Sugar Decorations

Frances McNaughton

Search Press

Contents

Introduction

The projects in this book are made using a number of techniques suitable for beginners to modelling in sugarpaste, with more detailed pieces, for those of you who are more advanced. The basic shapes and tools are kept as simple as possible and explained at the start of each section.

The amount of sugarpaste and the approximate conversions I have listed for each model are only intended as a guide; models can, of course, be made in different sizes.

White marzipan can be used to make most of the birds, animals and fairies, coloured in the same way as the sugarpaste. Chocolate sugarpastes and modelling pastes are a good way of making brown and cream models and parts without having to use food colours.

The techniques in this book can also be used to make long-lasting sugar decorations with non-edible modelling pastes such as the air-drying modelling pastes available from craft shops.

Sugar Birds

Basic materials

Non-stick 15cm (6in) rolling pin For rolling out sugarpaste or modelling paste.

Dogbone/ball tool For shaping and adding details on to the sugarpaste.

Dresden tool For shaping and adding details on to the sugarpaste.

Various cutters: heart cutters: 1cm (⅜in), 1.25cm (½in), 2.5cm (1in), garrett frill cutter; circle cutters: 1cm (⅜in), 2cm (¾in), 3.5cm (1½in), 4.5cm (1¾in), 6cm (2½in); square cutter: 2.5cm (1in) for cutting various shapes from sugarpaste.

Silicone multi-mould (including wings) This can be used to make the wings.

Small sharp-pointed scissors For adding detail and texture on to the sugarpaste.

Thin palette knife This is available from sugarcraft shops and art shops. It is useful for releasing sugarpaste from the work surface, and for cutting and marking lines.

Cutting wheel This is used for cutting shapes from rolled sugarpaste. A knife can also be used.

No. 2 piping tube This is for cutting tiny circles for eyes etc.

Soft paintbrush and water/ waterbrush This is used for dampening the sugarpaste to join pieces together, or for applying egg white.

Dusting brush This is used for applying edible powder food colour, or edible glitter.

Sugarpaste The paste I use is mainly commercially available coloured sugarpaste. White sugarpaste can also be coloured with strong edible food colours from sugarcraft shops and some supermarkets. It is not advisable to use liquid colours when making dark or bold colours as this could make the paste sticky and unworkable.

Modelling paste Some of the models need modelling paste – sugarpaste strengthened with CMC (cellulose gum) or gum tragacanth (250g/8oz sugarpaste to approximately half a teaspoon of the gum). This is used when parts need to dry harder e.g. long beaks and parts that need to stand. Leave for a few hours for the gum to develop before using.

When only a small amount of modelling paste is needed, simply knead small pinches of the gum into the sugarpaste.

Edible wafer paper For the wings on the Eagle and Cockatoo, and the wings and beak on the Hummingbird.

Other items

Non-stick workboard For modelling the sugarpaste on.

Sharp knife For cutting shapes from rolled sugarpaste.

Cocktail sticks Can be used instead of the Dresden tool for shaping and adding details on to the sugarpaste.

Small sieve/sugarcraft gun/ extruder These can be used to create very thin or fluffy looking strands of sugarpaste as for the pompom on the Robin's Christmas hat.

Ruler To measure out the size of sugarpaste and modelling paste.

Plastic sandwich bags For storing pieces of sugarpaste to keep them soft. Also, if you have problems rolling paste thinly, place the paste inside the plastic sandwich bag and then roll it.

Edible sugar candy sticks I have used commercially available edible sugar candy sticks in some of the models. If you are not able to buy these, or prefer to make your own, they can be made in advance at home. Make the modelling paste as above, then roll paste into thin sausage shapes and allow it to dry for a few days before using it.

Edible coloured dusting powder Available in plain and pearl colours, brushed on to the surface to add soft colour or an iridescent sheen.

Vegetable cooking oil To stop the paste sticking to your hands and tools, rub a small amount of this into your hands and the surface, or sprinkle a small amount of icing sugar instead. If using icing sugar, be careful not to use too much, as this could dry the paste and cause cracking.

A selection of the tools you will need.

9

Puffin

Instructions:

1 For the wings, roll out the black sugarpaste thinly. Using the heart cutter, cut out the heart shape and then cut it in half to make two wings.

2 For the eyes roll some black sugarpaste into two tiny balls.

3 Form the black sugarpaste into a 6cm (2½in) pointed cone for the body. Roll gently between your two fingers at the rounded end to make the neck and bend to stand the body up.

4 Roll out some white sugarpaste thinly. Using the heart cutter again, cut out two hearts and stick on one for the tummy, and one above it, slightly overlapping for the face.

5 Stick the two tiny black sugarpaste eyes and the wings in place.

6 Make a small pea-sized ball of blue sugarpaste, a smaller ball of yellow and an even smaller ball of red sugarpaste. Press them together to form the beak shape and stick the beak on to the head.

7 Roll two small pea-sized pieces of orange sugarpaste into cone shapes, and flatten slightly. Mark on three toes with the Dresden tool or a cocktail stick and attach them under the body.

Materials:

25g (just under 1oz)
black sugarpaste

Small pieces of white, orange, red,
yellow and blue sugarpaste

Tools:

Heart cutter: 2.5cm (1in)

Small rolling pin

Dresden tool/cocktail stick

Stick it on the Bill

*Who could resist making this
cute clown of the bird world?*

Penguin

2 ....

3

1

Instructions:

1 Roll out the black sugarpaste. Make a tiny ball of yellow sugarpaste and press it on to the black. Cut out a black square with the cutter, cutting through the yellow on the corner of the square – this will form the beak. Mark on two eyes with the piping tube.

2 For the penguin's body, shape a cone from the white sugarpaste. The length needs to be shorter than the diagonal of the square. Stand the cone up on its base.

3 Cover the cone with the black sugarpaste square with the yellow beak over the head first. The wings and tail can be left curved out or tweaked until the model resembles a penguin!

Materials:

10g (⅓oz) white sugarpaste
10g (⅓oz) black sugarpaste
Small amount of yellow sugarpaste

Tools:

Square cutter: 2.5cm (1in)
No. 2 piping tube

P-P-P-Pick Up a Penguin!

These sweet treats are as cool as ice, and a piece of cake to make!

Owl

Instructions:

1 To make the beak, form a tiny cone from brown sugarpaste.

2 For the two wings, model each from a large pea-sized piece of brown paste and make into a fat carrot shape. Flatten slightly and mark on the feathers using the Dresden tool.

3 To make the body, roll the main piece of brown sugarpaste into an oval shape, then roll it between your two fingers to form the neck and the head. Gently pinch and stroke the other end to form a short tail.

4 Cut out a heart from some thinly rolled-out white sugarpaste and stick on the body for a tummy. Use fine sharp-pointed scissors (with points towards the feet of the owl) to snip through the surface of the paste on the tummy to form lots of little spikes. Stroke the spikes downwards to look like feathers. When snipping with the scissors the underneath colour will then show.

14

5 Attach the wings to the sides of the body.

6 To make the face, roll out white paste thinly. Cut out a 2cm (¾in) and a 1cm (⅜in) circle. Cut each circle into quarters, attach one of the larger quarters for the chin and mark with the Dresden tool to suggest feathers. For the eye area, roll out some pale brown paste. Cut out a 2cm (¾in) circle and cut it into quarters. Stick two of the small white quarters to the pale brown ones. Stick on two small eyes made from two balls of black sugarpaste. Attach these two quarters and a plain quarter for the forehead, to the face. Mark the forehead with lines radiating outwards using the Dresden tool.

7 Attach the tiny brown beak.

8 Make two small pieces of white fluff by pressing some sugarpaste through a sieve, sugarcraft gun, or garlic press. Stick it on to the head to look like 'ears'.

Materials:

25g (just under 1oz) brown or chocolate sugarpaste

Small amounts of white, pale brown and black sugarpaste

Tools:

Small sharp-pointed scissors

Small sieve/sugarcraft gun

Heart cutter: 2.5cm (1in)

Circle cutters: 2cm (¾in) and 1cm (⅜in)

Small rolling pin

Dresden tool

As Wise as an Owl

Try using white sugarpaste instead of chocolate brown. When rolling out the paste for the tummy feathers, roll out white and pale brown, press together and roll again. Cut out the heart shape and stick to the tummy with the pale brown stuck to the body. When snipping with the scissors, the colour underneath will show.

Macaw

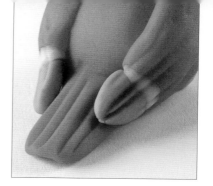

Materials:
- 25g (just under 1oz) red sugarpaste
- Small amounts of yellow, orange, blue and black sugarpaste
- Thin chocolate biscuit stick or candy stick for branch

Tools:
Sharp knife
Small sharp-pointed scissors
Dresden tool/cocktail stick
Heart cutter: 1.25cm (½in)

Instructions:

1 To make the feet, roll two small pea-sized balls of orange sugarpaste and model into small carrot shapes. Cut the pointed end into three toes or claws for the feet. Attach to the 'branch' (chocolate biscuit/candy stick).

2 For the wings take a large pea-sized amount of red, a smaller ball of blue and a tiny ball of yellow sugarpaste. Press them all together to form a cone shape with the blue paste at the tip of the wing. Mark on the lines for feathers using the Dresden tool,

and store them in a plastic bag to keep them soft until needed.

3 To make the body, roll the rest of the red paste to a pointed cone approximately 8cm (3in) long. Roll the cone between two fingers at the wide end to form a neck and a head. Bend the body to stand it up, and mark on the lines for the tail feathers with the Dresden tool.

4 Roll out some yellow sugarpaste thinly to make the face. Cut out a 1.25cm (½in) heart and attach two tiny black sugarpaste balls for the eyes. Make two very thin strands of black sugarpaste and

stick them to the yellow heart around the eyes. Cut the heart in half down the middle, and attach it to the head, leaving a small space in between for the beak.

5 For the beak, take a small pea-sized piece of yellow sugarpaste, and shape it to a fat cone. Make a smaller black cone and stick it under the yellow cone. Shape it to a curved beak and attach it to the front of the face.

6 Attach the wings to the body.

7 Dampen the tops of the feet and sit the macaw on top.

The Real Macaw

For a totally tropical cake topper, model these colourful parrots. Make the body in blue and the tip of the wings red as a fun variation.

Mallard

Instructions:

1 To make the body, form a 5cm (2in) cone of brown sugarpaste.

2 For the wings, place a tiny piece of blue sugarpaste at the tip of the wing feathers in the mould before putting in the grey sugarpaste. Stick the wings in place.

3 Take a small pea-sized ball of white sugarpaste and flatten slightly to make the collar. Stick on to the body.

4 For the head, roll a large pea-sized ball of green sugarpaste and stick it on top of the white collar. Attach tiny black eyes made from tiny balls of black sugarpaste.

5 To form the beak, roll a very small sausage of orange paste 1cm (⅜in) long. Dampen the front of the face and lay the orange sausage vertically. Press the middle of the beak inwards, folding it in the middle. Gently curl up the end of the top beak and mark two tiny nostrils where the beak joins the face.

Materials:

10g (⅓oz) brown sugarpaste

Small amounts of grey, orange, green, white, black and blue sugarpaste

Tools:

Wing mould

Dresden tool/cocktail stick

Ostrich

Materials:

Three white edible sugar candy sticks

10g (⅓oz) black modelling paste (see page 8)

25g (just under 1oz) green modelling paste

Small amounts of peach, white, black and orange sugarpaste

Tools:

Small sieve/sugarcraft gun

Dresden tool/cocktail stick

Small sharp-pointed scissors

Instructions:

1 Mould the green modelling paste to a drum shape for the base.

2 For the legs, use two edible sugar candy sticks. Stick a very small ball of orange paste two-thirds along each stick and flatten it slightly.

3 To make the feet, take two pea-sized pieces of orange sugarpaste and shape each to a small pointed cone. Cut through the pointed end of each twice to form three toes or claws. Attach the feet to the top of the green drum base. Push the legs straight down through the back of the feet until the stick touches the surface.

4 For the body, form the black modelling paste into a ball. Dampen the tops of the legs and push the body on, making sure it is vertical.

5 To make the head, attach a large pea-sized piece of peach sugarpaste to a sugar candy stick. Dampen the other end of the stick and carefully push it straight in to the body.

6 The beak is made from a very small cone of black sugarpaste which has been slightly flattened. This is then attached to the front of the head.

7 For the eyes, cut a tiny ball of black paste in half to make two pointed oval eyes. Stick them on to the face in line with the beak.

8 To make 'fluff', push small amounts of soft sugarpaste through a sieve or a sugarcraft gun. Attach it to the dampened head and body, pushing it into place with the point of the Dresden tool or a cocktail stick (do not press this on with your fingers as this could flatten it). The head should be peach all over, carefully avoiding the eyes and beak. The body should be black all over, and white around the base of the neck, with two little bits of white on each side for the tips of the wings.

Big Bird

I get lots of inspiration from toys and this big bird is modelled on those figures that wiggle when you push up from the base. It makes a quirky and hilarious cake topper.

Robin

Materials:
25g (just under 1oz) brown or chocolate sugarpaste

Small amounts of red, white and black sugarpaste

Tools:
Heart cutter: 2.5cm (1in)

Dresden tool/cocktail stick

No. 2 piping tube

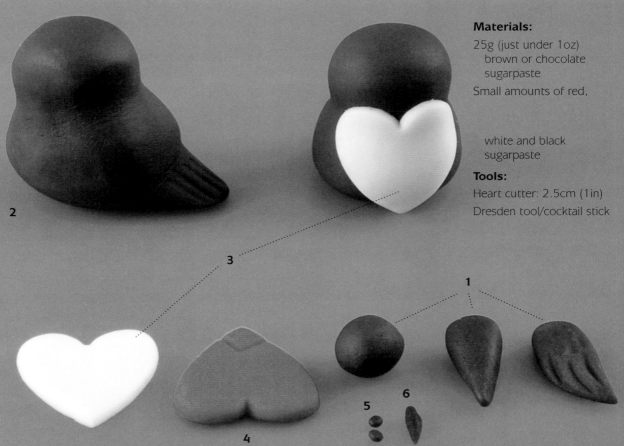

Materials:
25g (just under 1oz) brown or chocolate sugarpaste

Small amounts of red,

white and black sugarpaste

Tools:
Heart cutter: 2.5cm (1in)

Dresden tool/cocktail stick

Instructions:

1 Make two wings from two small pea-sized pieces of the brown sugarpaste rolled into cones. Mark with the Dresden tool for the feathers.

2 For the body, shape a pointed cone, 6cm (2½in) long, from brown sugarpaste. Roll the wide end gently between your two fingers to form a short, fat neck. Stand the model up by bending the tail back. Mark the feathers on the tail with the Dresden tool.

3 Cut out a white heart from some rolled-out white paste. Attach it to the body, point down.

4 Cut out a red heart from some rolled-out red paste. Cut the pointed end off with the pointed end of the heart cutter. Attach it upside down, above the white heart, overlapping.

5 Push the piping tube into the red heart on the head to form eye sockets. Make tiny eyes from balls of black sugarpaste and stick them into the eye sockets.

6 Make a tiny pointed beak from black sugarpaste and stick it in place.

Rocking Robin!

You're sure to be rocking around the Christmas tree with these two cuties on your cake! To make a more festive feathered friend, mark a line down the centre of the red heart, then mark on buttons with the piping tube. Make a cone of red paste and hollow the fat end slightly with your finger and thumb. Attach it to the top of the head and bend the point over to one side. Make white 'fluff' by pushing small amounts of sugarpaste through a sieve/sugarcraft gun. Attach the 'fluff' around the base and on the point of the hat to make a bobble.

Eagle

Instructions:

1 Using the wing template, trace the wing pattern on to edible wafer paper with the felt tip pen – make two. Carefully cut out the wings. Make the same marks to suggest feathers using the felt tip pen on both sides of each of the wings. Brush the brown edible powder colour from the edge of the wing inwards.

2 To make the body, form some brown sugarpaste into a cone. Attach a large pea-sized piece of white sugarpaste to the large end for the head. Use the tip of the Dresden tool to drag the surface of the two colours together forming a smooth feathered join. Continue to lengthen the cone shape to 8cm (3in), slightly thinner for the head and longer at the tail end. Bend the body to stand it up and shape and curve the head.

3 For the beak, shape a small piece of pale orange sugarpaste to a short pointed cone. Attach it to the head, curve the tip over and mark in the nostrils.

4 Make the eyes by rolling a tiny ball of black sugarpaste, and cut it in half to make two pointed ovals. Stick them on to the head.

5 To model the feet, shape two small cones of pale orange sugarpaste. Cut the pointed ends to make three toes or claws on each. Attach them under the body.

6 Dampen the back of the eagle and attach the wings.

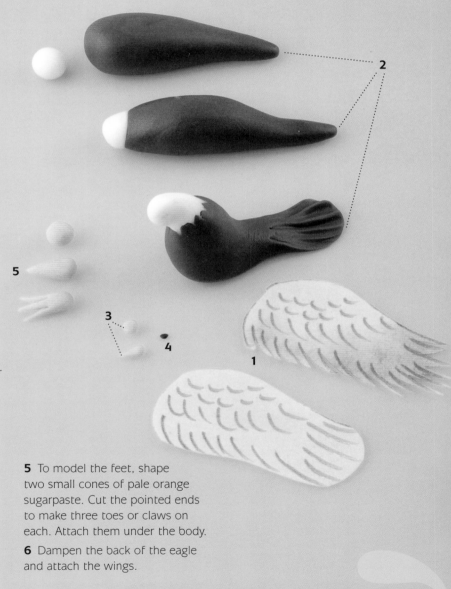

24

Materials:

- 25g (just under 1oz) brown or chocolate sugarpaste
- Small amounts of white, pale orange and black sugarpaste
- Edible wafer paper
- Food colour felt tip pen: brown
- Edible powder colour: brown

Tools:

- Dusting brush
- Dresden tool/ cocktail stick
- Sharp knife
- Wing template

The template for the wing, shown at actual size.

Bird's Eye View

Keep your eagle eye out for this big bird – with edible wafer paper wings, he's sure to fly off your guests' plates!

Cockatoo

Instructions:

1 Trace the wings on to the edible wafer paper using the template. Use the Dresden tool to keep the wafer paper white. Cut out the wings with scissors.

2 For the body, make an 8cm (3in) cone out of white sugarpaste. Roll the fat end between your two fingers to make the neck and the head. Mark on the tail feathers with the Dresden tool or a cocktail stick.

3 Make the beak out of a short cone of grey sugarpaste, attach it to the head and curve downwards. Mark on the two nostrils.

4 Make the eye sockets by pushing the piping tube into the sugarpaste head. Make two tiny balls of black sugarpaste and stick them into the eye sockets.

5 Shape a short cone of yellow sugarpaste for the crest. Cut into the pointed end, making at least three cuts. Attach it to the top of the head and curve the points upwards.

6 Make the feet from two small grey cones of sugarpaste. Cut the pointed end twice to form three toes or claws. Attach the feet to the candy stick, close together. Dampen the top of the feet and sit the body on top.

7 Dampen the sides of the body and attach the wings.

Spread Your Wings

Try your hand at modelling this popular pet in sugarpaste – no birdcage required!

Materials:

25g (just under 1oz) white sugarpaste

Small amounts of yellow, grey and black sugarpaste

Edible wafer paper

Chocolate stick or candy stick for the branch

Tools:

Wing template

Dresden tool/cocktail stick

Sharp knife/scissors

No. 2 piping tube

The template for the wing, shown at actual size.

Hummingbird

Instructions:

1 On edible wafer paper, draw two wings and a beak with the food colour felt tip pen, using the templates provided. Carefully cut them out. Turn the wafer paper wings over and draw the wings on the other side. Brush the Hummingbird's beak and wings with the dry edible powder colour in Deep Pink.

2 For the body, shape the purple sugarpaste to a 5cm (2in) long cone. Roll the wide end between your two fingers to form the neck, and cut out a 'V' shape for the tail. Bend the body to stand it up. With sharp-pointed scissors, mark two short vertical lines into the back for the wings and a short vertical line for the beak. Mark on two holes for the eye sockets using the no. 2 piping tube.

3 Brush edible powder pearl colour in Frosty Holly over the body.

4 Make two tiny eyes from black sugarpaste, dampen the eye sockets and stick them on.

5 Very lightly dampen the scissor marks and insert the beak and the wings.

28

Materials:

5g (⅙oz) purple sugarpaste

Small amount of black sugarpaste

Edible wafer paper

Edible powder colour: Deep Pink

Edible powder pearl colour:
    Frosty Holly

Food colour felt tip pen: purple

Tools:

Sharp-pointed scissors

Dusting brush

Sharp knife

No. 2 piping tube

The templates for the beak (left) and wing (below), shown at actual size.

This is Sure to Take Off

Try using different brightly-coloured sugarpaste and coloured pearl powders; such as blue sugarpaste with lilac pearl powder, red sugarpaste with gold powder or green sugarpaste with pink pearl powder. The shimmer really lifts your sugar creations.

Turkey

1

3

4

5

6

Materials:

25g (just under 1oz) brown or chocolate sugarpaste

25g (just under 1oz) red modelling paste (see page 8)

Small amounts of red, orange, blue and black sugarpaste

Tools:

Circle cutters: 6cm (2½in), 4.5cm (1¾in), 3.5cm (1½in)

Heart cutter: 1cm (³⁄₈in)

Dresden tool/cocktail stick

Wing mould

Cocktail stick

Instructions:

1 To make the tail, roll out red, orange and brown sugarpaste to about 3–4mm (⅛in) thick. Cut out the three circles – the largest in red paste, the medium in orange and the smallest in brown. Stick the circles on top of each other and cut off one end as shown. Drag the Dresden tool from the outer edge to the base repeatedly, forming a fan shape. Stand the tail up on its cut edge, curving it backwards.

2 Model two wings using brown sugarpaste. You can either use the wing mould or model them by hand: shape two small pea-sized pieces of sugarpaste into long cones and flatten them slightly. Mark on the feathers.

3 Shape the rest of the brown sugarpaste for the head and body by rolling one end of the ball of paste with your fingers to 5cm (2in) long. The neck should be approximately the same length as the fat body. Bend the neck up sharply to an 'S' shape.

4 To make the face, roll out the blue sugarpaste thinly and cut out a small heart. Stick it on to the front of the neck. Roll out some red sugarpaste thinly. Cut out the same size heart and mark a line down the centre. Attach it under the blue heart, point side up.

Dove Story

Make this fantail dove in the same way as the Turkey, but model the body in white sugarpaste and the beak in pink paste. Don't make the face parts, but for each eye make one tiny pink sugarpaste ball and one in black. Cut them in half to make pointed oval eyes, and attach the wings pointing down.

5 To make the eyes, take two tiny white balls of sugarpaste, and stick two tiny black sugarpaste balls to them. Stick them on to the blue face.

6 Roll a tiny brown pointed cone of sugarpaste for the beak. Stick it on, and mark on the nostrils with a cocktail stick. Roll a tiny strand of red paste and attach above the beak, positioning it so that it hangs down on one side.

7 Attach the body to the front of the tail, and stick the wings on to the sides of the body, with the tips of the wings pointing down.

Rooster

Instructions:

1 For the tail feathers, roll some small pea-sized balls of the red, green and purple modelling paste. Form each of them into a thin cone approximately 2cm (¾in) long. Dampen the fat ends and press gently together with the tips fanning out. Curve the tips all in the same direction. Leave to dry for a few hours.

2 To make the base, form a fat cube of the black paste. Make a hole in the centre of the cube using the dry candy stick and remove it.

3 Make six very thin, tiny cones of orange sugarpaste for the feet. Stick them to the top of the base.

4 For the body, form a pointed oval of purple sugarpaste 5cm (2in) long. Dampen the surface and lay a candy stick across the centre. Fold the purple sugarpaste in half, bringing the points together and keeping the candy stick stuck inside, with each end sticking out of the paste. Curve the pointed end upwards for the tail.

5 To make the head, shape the yellow sugarpaste into a sausage 3cm (1¼in) long. Insert a dry candy stick lengthwise, almost to the end and then remove the stick. Pinch out the open end to

Cock-a-Doodle-Doo!

Wakey wakey! It's time to start sugarcrafting this farmyard favourite! Use more earthy shades of sugarpaste for the body, wings and tail, and lose the red comb and wattle to make a brood of hens to join your Rooster.

widen it. Cut into the widened edge with scissors to make a zigzag edge. Dampen the inside edge of the paste and attach the head to the body over the stick. Make two small eyes from the black sugarpaste and stick them on. Flatten a 1cm (³/₈in) sausage of red sugarpaste, dampen along the top of the head, attach the red paste and make indentations with the Dresden tool or a cocktail stick for the Rooster's comb.

6 Stick a very small orange cone on for the beak and cut across the middle with scissors to open it. Make two very small thin cones of red paste and attach them to the front of the face, just under the beak.

7 Dampen the candy stick and push the Rooster into the base, making sure it's vertical.

8 For the wings, take two pea-sized pieces of purple sugarpaste and shape each into a cone, flatten, and mark on feathers with the Dresden tool or cocktail stick. Dampen them and attach them to the body, leaving the tips of the wings slightly apart. Dampen the base of the tail feathers and press them between the tips of the wings to attach them.

Materials:

White edible sugar candy stick

25g (just under 1oz) black modelling paste (see page 8)

Small amounts of red, green, orange, purple and black modelling paste

10g (¹/₃oz) purple sugarpaste

5g (¹/₆oz) yellow sugarpaste

Tools:

Sharp-pointed scissors

Dresden tool/cocktail stick

Edible sugar candy stick to use for modelling

Kingfisher

Instructions:

1 Make a pair of wings in the mould, or shape them by hand in blue sugarpaste.

2 Form a 6cm (2½in) cone-shaped body from the blue sugarpaste. Make the neck by rolling the fat end between your two fingers, and bend the body to sit up. Shape the head to a slight point and stroke the top of the head to make it slightly flatter. Attach the wings. Brush the Kingfisher's body and wings with the edible powder pearl colour.

3 Shape two 1.5cm (½in) long white sugarpaste cones, and two in orange, the same size. Stick the orange on to the white, as shown. Flatten them slightly and attach them to the head, points forward.

34

Materials:

25g (just under 1oz)
  blue sugarpaste

Small amounts of orange
  and white sugarpaste

Small amount of black modelling
  paste (see page 8)

Edible powder pearl colour:
  Glacier Blue

Tools:

Wing mould

Dusting brush

No. 2 piping tube

Heart cutter: 2.5cm (1in)

Sharp-pointed scissors

Take the Plunge

Reach for your edible pearl colour powder to add a shimmer to this blue beauty of the bird world.

Woodpecker

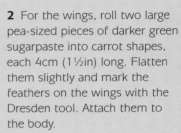

Instructions:

1 To make the body, roll the pale green sugarpaste to a pointed cone approximately 8cm (3in) long. Roll it between your two fingers to form the neck at the rounded end, and shape it so that the head is up and the body and tail are straight. Mark some feathers on the tail with the Dresden tool.

2 For the wings, roll two large pea-sized pieces of darker green sugarpaste into carrot shapes, each 4cm (1½in) long. Flatten them slightly and mark the feathers on the wings with the Dresden tool. Attach them to the body.

3 To make the beak and mask, form some black modelling paste into a 3cm (1¼in) long cone. At the fat end, make a cut to form a 'Y' and shape the cut ends to form points, keeping the total length at 3cm (1¼in). Dampen inside the top of the 'Y' and stick it to the front of head, smoothing the side pieces in to look like a mask, with the point forming the beak.

4 Make two tiny balls each of white and black sugarpaste for the eyes. Stick the black on top of the white, and then attach them to the mask.

5 Make a small pea-sized ball of red sugarpaste, then shape and flatten it to a long, slightly rounded triangle. Attach on to the top of the head for the bird's crown.

36

Materials:

25g (just under 1oz) pale green
    sugarpaste

Small amounts of darker green and
    red sugarpaste

Small amount of black
    modelling paste (see page 8)

Tools:

Dresden tool/cocktail stick

Spotted Our Woodpecker?

To make a Spotted Woodpecker, make the body in white and the wings in black. Lay thin strips of white across the pointed ends of the wings for stripes and press in. Mark the feathers as before.

Sugar Animals

Basic tools

Heart cutter, 2.5cm (1in)
For cutting out faces.

Tiny blossom cutter
For cutting out the Leopard's spots (see pages 50–51).

Cocktail stick/toothpick
For making marks and shaping small pieces of sugarpaste.

Sharp-pointed scissors
For cutting sugarpaste.

Drinking straw, cut off at an angle
This is used to make curved marks for mouths and other details.

Thin palette knife
This is available from sugarcraft and art shops. It is useful for releasing sugarpaste from the work surface, and for cutting and marking lines.

Other equipment

Small paintbrush or water brush Used for dampening the sugarpaste to join pieces together.

Vegetable cooking oil
To stop paste sticking to your hands and tools, rub a small amount of oil in to your hands and work surface.

Icing sugar Alternatively, sprinkle a small amount of icing sugar on your hands and work surface. Be careful not to use too much, as this could dry the paste and cause cracking.

Plastic sandwich bags
For storing pieces of paste to keep them soft, and for rolling paste flat, as for the Leopard's spots (see page 50–51).

Non-stick workboard

Small rolling pin

Joining shapes

Join the pieces of each model together as they are made, while still soft, by dampening the surfaces with a small paintbrush dipped in water. Try not to over-wet the paste or the pieces will slide off rather than stick.

Basic shapes

1 Ball

It is a good idea to start each shape by making a smooth ball shape first. Knead the paste until smooth and roll it between the palms of your hands to shape a ball with no visible cracks.

2 Oval or egg shape

Roll the ball in the palms of your hands to make it longer.

3 Cone

Roll the ball at one end in the palms of your hands.

4 Pear (used for some of the heads)

Roll the ball at one end between your fingers.

5 Sausage

Roll the ball with your hands to make the sausage.

6 Round-ended sausage

(used for some of the legs) Roll one side of the ball to make a sausage, leaving one end fatter.

7 Long, pointed oval

(used for some of the bodies) Roll the ball to form two narrow ends.

8 Carrot

Roll the ball to form a long, pointed cone.

9 Candy stick (used as a support)

These can be bought from sweet shops. When the packet is first opened, the candy sticks can be a bit too soft, so lay them out to dry for a few days, until hard. They can also be made in advance from strengthened sugarpaste: knead a pinch of CMC into 50g (1¾oz) of sugarpaste. Roll to form thin sausages and cut to 6cm (2½in). Leave to dry in a warm, dry place for a few days, until hard.

Panda

Instructions:

1 Divide the white paste into about 25g (just under 1oz) for the body, 10g (⅓oz) for the head and a pea-sized piece for the cheeks and eyes.

2 Make the body into an egg shape with a candy stick for support (not shown).

3 Divide the black paste into four balls: two for the legs, one for the arms and one for the face, nose, ears, eyes and tail.

4 For the legs, form two of the black balls into pear shapes. Shape a foot at the fat end. Mark claws with a cocktail stick. Attach the narrow end of each leg to the main body.

5 For the arms, make one long sausage from the other black ball. Stick on top of the body.

6 Make the head from a ball of white paste, approximately half the size of the body.

7 Cut out a black heart shape for the face, using the heart cutter.

8 Attach an oval of white on to the heart shape. Mark two curves, side by side, for the mouth, using a drinking straw.

9 Make a black triangle for the panda's nose.

10 For the eyes, press two tiny balls of white and then two even

smaller balls of black on to the heart shape. Stick the face on to the head. Attach the head on to the top of the body.

11 For the ears, make two small balls of black paste and shape them to make indents.

12 Make the tail from a small ball of black paste.

13 Stick on three small pink balls to each foot for the toe pads, and a larger one for the sole of the foot.

Materials:

35g (1¼oz) white sugarpaste
30g (1oz) black sugarpaste
Tiny piece of pink sugarpaste
Candy stick

Tools:

Cocktail stick
Drinking straw
Sharp-pointed scissors
Thin palette knife
Heart cutter, 2.5cm (1in)

Mama Panda

The baby panda is just a smaller version of its mum, lying in a more relaxed position. It has a pink nose to make it extra cute.

Lizard

Instructions:

1 Set aside a tiny piece of the black paste for the eyes.

2 Make the legs from four large pea-sized pieces of blue paste rolled into sausage shapes. Bend each to form a knee and foot. Cut each foot with scissors to form three toes.

3 For the body, join the main ball of black paste to the remaining ball of blue paste and roll to form a long carrot shape. The blue end should form a point. Roll the black end between your fingers to form a neck and head. Flatten the nose end slightly. Mark nostrils with a cocktail stick.

4 Attach the legs on to the underside of the body, feet pointing forward.

5 Roll two thin yellow sausages, slightly shorter than the body. Stick on top of the body to look like stripes.

6 For the eyes, make two small balls of red paste, and two smaller balls of black and stick together on to the sides of the head.

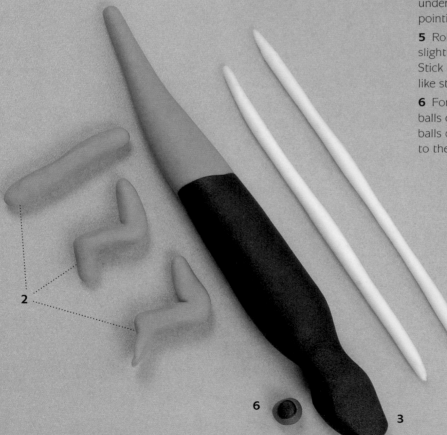

Materials:
15g (½oz) black sugarpaste
10g (⅓oz) blue sugarpaste
Pea-sized piece of yellow sugarpaste
Tiny pieces of red and black sugarpaste

Tools:
Cocktail stick
Sharp-pointed scissors

Snakes

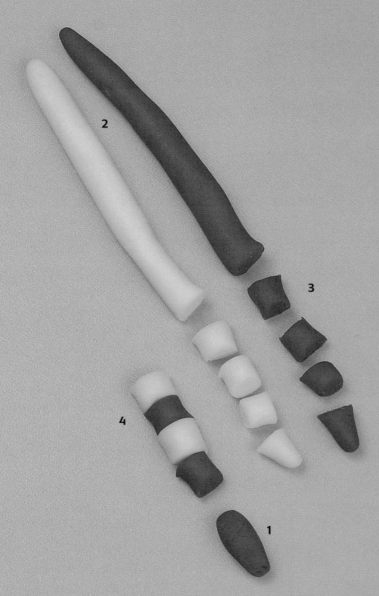

Instructions:

1 For the head, make a small cone shape and flatten the narrow end. Mark the nostrils with a cocktail stick. Attach two tiny black eyes (not shown).

2 Roll two or three different colours of paste into thin sausages.

3 Cut each sausage into small segments. Join the different-coloured segments back together to form stripes.

4 Roll gently with your hand to form a smooth sausage for the body with a thin point for the tail. Shape the body by bending or coiling it up.

5 Attach the head.

Materials:
Large pea-sized pieces of red,
   yellow and black sugarpaste

Tools:
Thin palette knife
Cocktail stick

Dolphin

Materials:

- 15g (½oz) each of blue and pale blue sugarpaste
- Tiny piece of black sugarpaste

Tools:

- Sharp-pointed scissors or thin palette knife
- Cocktail stick

2

3

1

4

6

Instructions:

1 For the fins, shape three small pea-sized pieces of blue paste into small carrot shapes. Flatten and curve them slightly.

2 Make a smooth ball from the blue paste and one from the pale blue paste. Roll each between your hands to form pointed sausage shapes. Join them gently together by rolling.

3 Roll one end of the dolphin between your fingers to form the narrow nose. To make the tail, roll the other end of the dolphin between your fingers and flatten it slightly.

4 Cut into the centre of the flattened end about 1cm (⅜in) with the scissors or knife. Flatten and shape the points of the tail.

5 Attach one of the fins on the back and one on each side. Curve the tips towards the tail. Mark a blowhole with a cocktail stick.

6 Make the eyes from two tiny balls of black paste and attach them.

Stay Close!
Make a baby dolphin to swim alongside its mother, using purple sugarpaste.

Kangaroo

Instructions:

1 Divide the orange paste in two and use about half for the body. Shape a ball of paste in the palm of your hand to form a long, fat carrot shape. Roll one end to make a long, pointed tail. Bend the body to make it stand up. Push in a candy stick to support the head (not shown). Divide the rest of the orange paste into: a large pea-sized ball for the arms and another piece. Divide the other piece into three for the legs, arms and head.

2 For the tummy, make a flattened oval of white paste and attach it to the body.

3 To make the legs, roll two balls of the orange paste between your fingers to leave a fat end. Flatten the fat end and mark toes at the thin end with a knife. Roll the fat end towards the thin end and attach the legs to the body.

4 For the arms, roll one small sausage. Mark the paws at each end using a cocktail stick. Stick the arms on top of the body.

5 To make the ears, break off a tiny piece of paste and make two small carrot shapes. Flatten them in the middle with a cocktail stick.

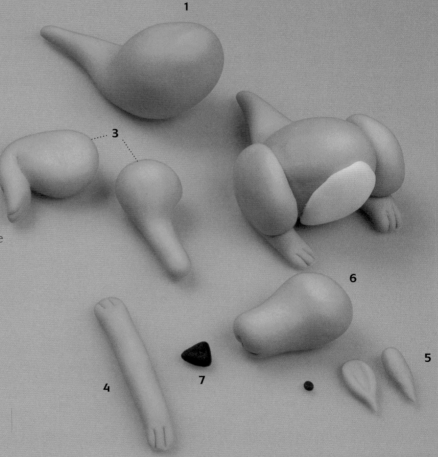

6 Use a ball of orange paste to make a pear shape for the head. At the narrow end, mark the mouth with a drinking straw.

7 Make the nose from a small triangle of black paste.

8 Make the eyes from two tiny black balls of paste. Attach the eyes and nose to the head.

9 Attach the head to the body. Stick the ears on to the back of the head.

Materials:
50g (1¾oz) orange sugarpaste
Pea-sized piece of white sugarpaste
Tiny piece of black sugarpaste
Candy stick

Tools
Thin palette knife
Cocktail stick
Drinking straw

Hey Joey

The baby kangaroo is made from yellow sugarpaste in a smaller size, and he is in a slightly different position to make him look inquisitive!

Leopard

Instructions:

1 Divide the pale lemon paste, taking about 25g (just under 1oz) for the body. Form this into a long, pointed oval. Cut into the ends, to make the legs.

2 Bend the back legs under the body. Smooth the cut edges. Mark toes. Push in a short candy stick (not shown) at the top of the front legs, to support the head. Divide the rest of the paste into about 10g (⅓oz) for the head and 5g (⅙oz) for the tail.

3 Form the tail piece into a long sausage and roll a tiny black piece into the end. Attach the tail to the body.

4 Form the head from a ball.

5 Form two small white ovals for the cheeks and attach these. For the ears, make two small balls

of brown and two smaller balls of white. Press the white gently on to the brown. Dampen the head and stick the ears on.

6 Add a small black triangle for the nose and two tiny black eyes.

7 Join the head on to the body at the top of the front legs.

8 Roll out brown sugarpaste with a small rolling pin. If you roll the paste inside a plastic sandwich

bag, it can be rolled quite thinly without sticking to the rolling pin or surface.

9 Cut out tiny brown blossoms with the cutter. Stick them all over the leopard.

50

Materials:

40g (1⅓oz) pale lemon or ivory sugarpaste (you could use white chocolate or marzipan)

Small amounts of white, brown and black sugarpaste

Candy stick

Tools:

Small rolling pin and plastic sandwich bag

Tiny blossom cutter

Cocktail stick

Thin palette knife

Sharp-pointed scissors

Basking

This leopard is stretching out with a little cub, made in exactly the same way, using smaller amounts of sugarpaste.

Racoon

Instructions:

1 Divide the grey paste in half. Use one half to make a long, pointed oval for the body. Cut into the ends to make the legs.

2 Bend the back legs under the body. Smooth the cut edges. Mark the toes. Divide the rest of the grey into two pieces – one for the head, one for the tail.

3 For the tail, make two thin sausages, grey and black. Cut them into small segments, place them in alternate colours and join them back together. Roll gently to make a smooth, striped tail. Join on to the back end of the body.

4 To make the head, form a ball into a slightly triangular shape.

5 Make two small white cones and two smaller black cones and press them on to the face to look a like a mask.

6 To make the cheeks, stick on a small ball of white and mark with a drinking straw.

7 Attach a small black triangle for the nose.

8 To make the eyes, press on two tiny flattened balls of white and two smaller balls of black on top.

9 Join the head on to the body at the top of the front legs.

10 Make the ears from two small grey cones. Indent the middle with a cocktail stick. Attach to the head.

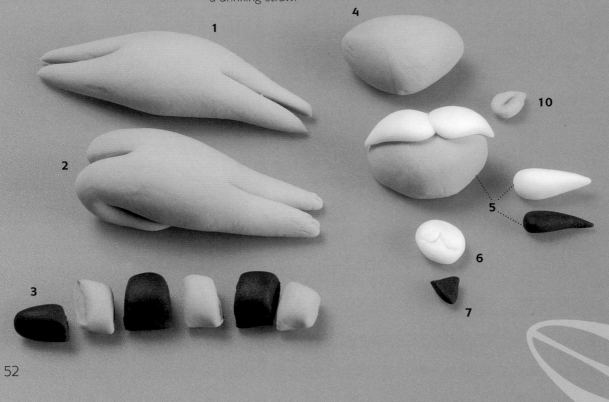

52

Materials:

20g (⅔oz) grey sugarpaste

Small amounts of black and white sugarpaste

Tools

Fine palette knife

Drinking straw

Cocktail stick

Koala

Instructions:

1 Divide the lilac sugarpaste, taking about 25g (just under 1oz) for the body, then form this into an egg shape and add a candy stick for support (not shown). Stick on a white heart shape for the tummy. Divide the rest of the lilac paste into four balls.

2 Take two of the balls and form each one into a carrot shape to make the legs. Mark toes with a knife. Attach the legs.

3 Divide one of the balls into two and make smaller carrot shapes for the arms. Mark the paws with a knife. Join the arms to the body.

4 The last lilac ball makes the head. Mark the mouth with a drinking straw. Attach the head to the body.

5 Make two small white ovals for the ears. Stick on the sides of the head, pushing in gently to cup them. Snip around the edges using sharp-pointed scissors.

6 Make the nose from a black oval shape and the eyes from two tiny balls of black paste.

Materials:

65g (2¼oz) lilac sugarpaste

Small amounts of white and black
sugarpaste

Candy stick

Tools:

Drinking straw

Sharp-pointed scissors

Thin palette knife

Heart cutter, 2.5cm (1in)

G'day!

*The little koala is made in
white with a lilac tummy, and
seems to be waving a paw!*

Lion

9

5

2

7

6

3

Materials:

- 50g (1¾oz) golden yellow sugarpaste
- 15g (½oz) orange sugarpaste
- Small amounts of black and brown sugarpaste
- Candy stick

Tools:

- Cocktail stick
- Sharp-pointed scissors
- Thin palette knife
- Heart cutter, 2.5cm (1in)

4

Instructions:

1 Divide the yellow paste, taking about 25g (just under 1oz) for the body. Form this into an egg shape and add a candy stick for support. Divide the rest of the paste into about 5g (1/6oz) each for the front legs, tail and face, and the rest for the back legs.

2 Form the piece for the back legs into two cones. Flatten them slightly, mark toes with a cocktail stick and join them on to the body.

3 For the front legs, attach two sausage shapes, the same height as the body. Mark lines on the end of each foot to form paws.

4 To make the mane, form a ball of orange paste and squash it slightly to make a fat circle. Mark soft indents around the edge with a cocktail stick. Attach it to the top of the body.

5 For the face, cut out a heart shape from yellow paste, using the heart cutter. Save a small piece of paste for the ears. Stick the heart shape on to the mane.

6 Make the cheeks from two small yellow ovals. Mark them with a cocktail stick for the whiskers and attach them to the heart-shaped face.

7 Form the nose from a small triangle of brown paste and the eyes from two tiny balls of black paste. Attach these to the face.

8 Make the ears from two small balls of yellow paste. Stick them on to the head, cupping them at the same time.

9 Make a long, thin sausage for the tail. Flatten one end slightly, then cut with a knife or scissors to make the end look fluffy. Attach the tail.

Pride

The lioness is made in the same way, but the head is made from a yellow ball as she does not have a mane.

Monkey

Instructions:

1 Divide the brown paste, taking about 35g (1¼oz) to make an egg shape for the body. A hardened candy stick can be pushed right into the body, leaving a small piece at the top to help support the head.

2 Make a thin sausage of brown paste for the tail. Coil up the end and attach to the bottom of the body.

3 Take a pea-sized piece of brown paste for the ears and press a smaller ball of peach on top. Cut in half across the top. Divide the rest of the brown paste into five equal balls.

4 Make four of the brown balls into long sausages for the legs and arms. Bend each in the middle for the knees and elbows.

5 Make four hands from small peach-coloured cones. Flatten slightly, and cut one long thumb and four fingers on each. Make two left- and two right-handed.

6 Attach the legs and arms to the body. Stick on the hands.

7 Take the fifth brown ball for the head and attach it to the body. Position the arms as shown.

8 Dampen the cut edge of the ears and attach to the side of the head.

9 For the face, cut out a heart shape in peach, using the heart cutter. Stick a small oval of peach at the bottom of the heart. Mark a wide mouth with a knife. Mark nostrils with a cocktail stick.

10 Stick on eyes made from two tiny balls of black and attach the face to the head.

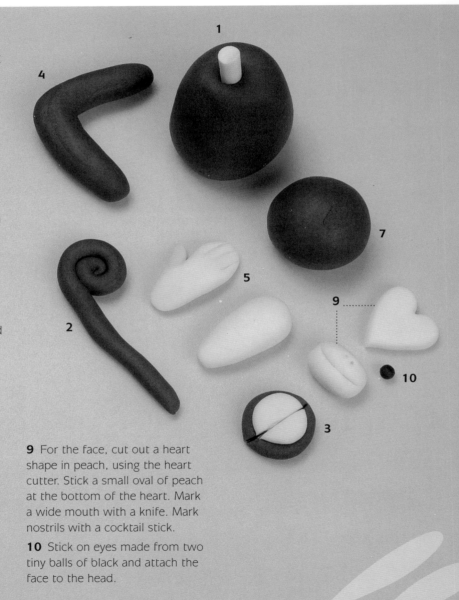

Materials:

100g (3½oz) brown or
    chocolate sugarpaste

20g (⅔oz) peach sugarpaste

Small amount of black sugarpaste

Candy stick

Tools:

Cocktail stick

Sharp-pointed scissors

Thin palette knife

Heart cutter, 2.5cm (1in)

Hippopotamus

Instructions:

1 Divide the paste; about 15g (½oz) for the head and ears, and 35g (1¼oz) for the body. To make the body, shape a ball of purple paste in the palm of your hand to form a long oval.

2 Cut into the narrow ends to make the legs.

3 Bend the whole body to form a curve, and to stand upright on the legs. Push a candy stick in at the top of the front legs to support the head (not shown).

4 Snip a small tail with scissors.

5 For the head, break off a tiny piece of paste and save it to make the ears. Make a fat pear shape for the head. Mark two nostrils, and mark the mouth using a knife.

6 For the eyes, make two tiny, flattened balls of white, and press on two smaller balls of black. Stick on to the face.

7 Attach the head on to the body.

8 Make two tiny balls for the ears from the remaining purple sugarpaste. Shape the indents and attach the ears to the head.

2

3

4

5

8

6

Materials:
50g (1¾oz) purple sugarpaste
Tiny pieces of white and black sugarpaste
Candy stick

Tools:
Thin palette knife
Sharp-pointed scissors
Cocktail stick

Tiger

1

8

5

3, 4

6

10

9

6

2, 4

Materials:

35g (1¼oz) orange sugarpaste

Small pieces of black, white and
   pink sugarpaste

Candy stick

Tools:

Fine palette knife

Cocktail stick

Heart cutter, 2.5cm (1in)

Sharp-pointed scissors

Instructions:

1 Divide the orange paste, taking about 20g (⅔oz) for the body. Make a long, pointed oval. Cut into the ends to make the legs. Smooth the cut edges. Mark the toes with a cocktail stick. Push in a short candy stick (not shown) at the top of the front legs to support the head. Divide the rest of the paste into a large pea size for the tail, and what is left for the head.

2 Make the tail from a long sausage with a black piece rolled into the end.

3 Make a ball for the head.

4 Make stripes from black sugarpaste by rolling thin, pointed sausages 2cm (¾in) long. Stick them across the body, legs, tail and head. Attach the tail to the body.

5 For the face, cut out a black heart with the heart cutter and flatten the edge slightly to widen it. Cut out a white heart and press on top of the black one, so the edge of the black shows. Stick on to the head.

6 Attach two small white ovals for the cheeks, a small black triangle for the nose, and two tiny black eyes. Use a cocktail stick to mark whiskers in the cheeks.

7 Stick the head on to the body at the top of the front legs.

8 For the ears, make two small balls of black and two smaller balls of white. Press the white gently on to the black.

9 Make two small sausages of white and flatten along the edges. Join the fat edge down the sides of the head. Make snips along the edges using the scissors to make them look fluffy.

10 To make the back paws, make two small balls of pink. On each one, press three tiny pink balls for the toes. Stick into place.

Crocodile

Instructions:

1 Make four pea-sized pieces for the feet. Roll each to make a small cone. Flatten slightly. Mark the toes with a knife.

2 To make the eyes, take one small pea-sized piece of green, press on a slightly smaller ball of white, then press on an even smaller ball of black. Cut the whole ball in half across the top.

3 Use the rest of the green paste to form a long pointed carrot shape for the body. The pointed end will form the tail. Roll the fatter end of the body between your fingers to form the head, and flatten it slightly.

4 Mark the mouth with a knife, and make two nostrils by pressing in the point of a cocktail stick.

5 Use scissors to mark small 'v' shapes down the crocodile's back.

6 Join the legs to the sides of the body.

7 Stick the cut edges of the eyes on top of the head.

Materials:

50g (1¾oz) green sugarpaste

Small amounts of white and black sugarpaste

Tools:

Cocktail stick

Drinking straw

Sharp-pointed scissors

Thin palette knife

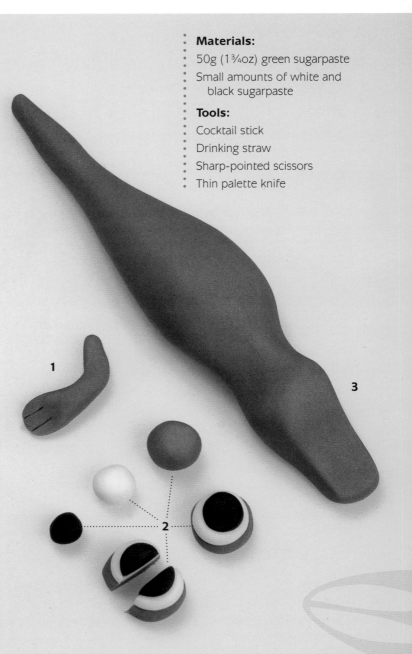

Frog

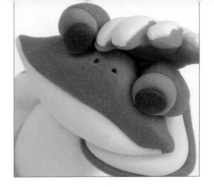

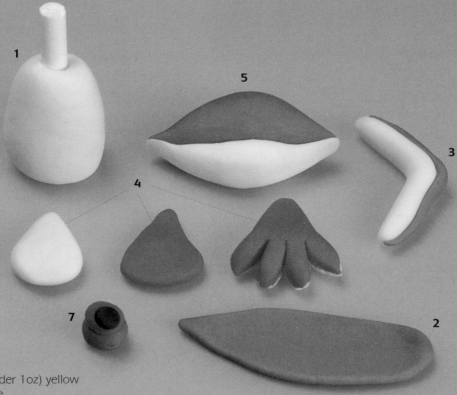

Materials:

- 25g (just under 1oz) yellow sugarpaste
- 15g (½oz) green sugarpaste
- Small amounts of red and black sugarpaste
- Candy stick

Tools:

- Cocktail stick
- Sharp-pointed scissors
- Thin palette knife
- Plastic sandwich bag

Instructions:

1 For the body, make a narrow oval from 15g (½oz) of yellow paste. Push in a candy stick slightly longer than the body, as support.

2 Make the back from a thin oval of green paste. Roll it slightly longer than the body and stick on to the body, leaving a short point for the stumpy tail.

3 For the legs and arms, make four small balls of yellow and four smaller balls of green. Roll each to form long sausage shapes. Stick the green and yellow together and roll again to make it smooth. Bend each sausage in the middle. Stick two on to the bottom of the body for legs, and two on the top, for arms.

4 For the hands and feet, make four small balls of yellow and four balls of red. Form each to a simple triangle and flatten. Stick the red triangles to the yellow ones. Cut to form four fingers and smooth the cut edges with your fingers. Put the hands and feet into a plastic sandwich bag to stay soft.

5 Make a long oval of green for the head, and a smaller long oval of yellow. Press together and roll each end to a point. Stick the head on top of the body. Mark two little nostrils with a cocktail stick. Position the arms while they are still soft.

6 Stick the hands and feet in position.

7 For the eyes, make two small pea-sized pieces of green. Stick a slightly smaller ball of red on each. Then stick on an even smaller ball of black. Stick the eyes on top of the head.

Sugar Fairies

Basic materials

I made my fairies in **sugarpaste**, coloured with **strong paste food colours**. Ready-coloured sugarpaste, **modelling paste**, and the other items you will need are available from specialist sugarcraft shops and online sugarcraft and cake decorating suppliers. A stronger type of modelling paste can be made by kneading a small pinch of **CMC** (cellulose gum), or gum tragacanth into sugarpaste. This stronger paste is used for some of the wings and for the standing models, and can also be used for making candy sticks for the legs and supports.

For many of the fairies, I used 'candy sticks', available from sweet shops, for the arms, legs and neck supports. I also used **chocolate-covered biscuit sticks** and **liquorice sticks** in different flavours.

Clockwise from left in the picture, **various cutters**: an eight-petal flower cutter, a carnation cutter, a calyx (five-point) cutter, a variety of butterfly cutters, a garrett frill cutter (large, fluted round cutter), circle cutters, an oak leaf cutter, a heart cutter, a tiny blossom cutter and a daisy cutter.

Multi-mould This can be used to make a tiny crown, wings, a tiny flower, a tiny faceted star and other small items useful for making fairies.

Small drinking straw This should be cut off at an angle, and is used for making the fairies' mouths and closed eyes.

Cocktail stick This is used for shaping and texturing techniques.

Various tools: a textured frilling tool, a dogbone tool and a Dresden tool.

Cutting wheel This is used for cutting shapes from rolled sugarpaste.

Thin palette knife This is available from sugarcraft shops and art shops. It is useful for releasing sugarpaste from the work surface, and for cutting and marking lines.

Dusting brush This is used for applying edible powder food colour, or edible glitter.

Black or brown **food colour felt-tip pen** This is used for making edible marks.

Small paintbrush/ water brush This is used for dampening the sugarpaste to join pieces together, or for applying egg white.

Small non-stick rolling pin This is for rolling out sugarpaste or modelling paste.

Small plain piping tubes These are for cutting tiny circles for eyes.

Various edible pearl colours and **edible glitter** (shown right) These are used to add a sparkle to fairies.

Other items

To stop paste sticking to your hands and tools, rub a small amount of **vegetable cooking oil** in to your hands and the surface, or sprinkle a small amount of icing sugar. If using icing sugar, be careful not to use too much, as this could dry the paste and cause cracking.

Use **plastic sandwich bags** for storing pieces of sugarpaste. Also, if you have problems rolling paste thinly, place the paste inside the plastic sandwich bag and then roll it.

A **sieve, sugarcraft gun** or **garlic press** can be used to create very thin or fluffy looking strands of sugarpaste as for the pompoms for the Christmas Fairy.

Materials for joining sugarpaste shapes

Most parts can be stuck together just by dampening them with water. Make sure that the paste is only dampened – don't wet the surface too much, or the pieces will just slide off. Fresh egg white can also be used as a slightly stickier glue. You can also use thick edible glue. This is useful for attaching dried sugar pieces (for instance the wings and heads) and for when a stronger glue is needed. Mix a pinch of modelling paste with a few drops of water by mashing it with a palette knife until it forms a stringy, sticky glue. If you make this glue with the same colour paste as used on the model, it will be easier to hide.

Rainbow Fairy

Materials:

10g (⅓oz) flesh-coloured sugarpaste

10g (⅓oz) blue sugarpaste

10g (⅓oz) blue modelling paste (see page 68)

10g (⅓oz) each red, yellow, purple and green sugarpaste

Three candy sticks

Tiny amount of black sugarpaste

Thick edible glue

Tools:

Tiny blossom cutter

Small drinking straw

Thin palette knife

Non-stick rolling pin

Circle cutters: 22mm (⅞in), 32mm (1¼in), 41mm (1⅝in), 56mm (2¼in)

Plastic sandwich bag

Water brush

Dresden tool or cocktail stick

Scrunched-up paper tissue

Instructions:

1 For the head, take the flesh-coloured sugarpaste and pinch off a piece. Use this to make two tiny teardrop shapes for the ears and a tiny pin-head piece for the nose. Form the rest into a ball and use a finger to roll a slight indentation across the middle. Make a hole in the neck end using a dry candy stick. Attach the nose in the centre of the face, and press a mouth shape with the cut drinking straw under the nose. Dampen the sides of the head in line with the nose. Stick the ears on and press in place using a Dresden tool or cocktail stick, forming the ear shape. Make two tiny pin-head size pieces of black sugarpaste for the eyes. Dampen the face to stick them on, slightly above the nose.

2 For the wings, roll out the blue modelling paste and cut it with the largest circle cutter. Roll out the green, red and yellow pastes, and cut them using a smaller size of circle cutter for each one. Dampen the surface of the blue circle and attach the green one, then dampen and attach the red, then the yellow. Cut the circle into quarters (this makes two pairs of wings) and leave to dry for a few hours or overnight.

3 Make the shoes with two pea-sized pieces of coloured sugarpaste. Shape to form a point. Dampen the ends of two of the candy sticks and attach the shoes.

4 Make an egg shape of the blue sugarpaste for the body with a candy stick for support, slightly sticking out. Push the legs into the body.

5 Make coloured petals for the skirt using pea-sized pieces of sugarpaste, flattened and thinned at the edge by pressing them in a plastic sandwich bag. Attach the petals around the body.

6 Take a slightly larger than pea-sized piece of coloured sugarpaste for each arm. Roll to form a long carrot shape, shorter than the legs. Flatten the thin end, and cut a little thumb to make the hand. Position the arms and attach them to the body.

7 For the hair, make lots of small carrot-shaped pieces of different coloured sugarpaste. Dampen the head and attach the strands of hair with the pointed end towards the face and neck. When the head is covered with enough strands of hair, cut out some tiny blossoms in different colours and stick on to the top of the head.

8 Dampen the end of the candy stick neck and attach the head, looking to one side.

9 Attach the wings with thick edible glue (see page 69). Prop them up with scrunched-up paper tissue until the glue is dry.

Rose Fairy

Materials:

10g (⅓oz) flesh-coloured
   sugarpaste

20g (⅔oz) red sugarpaste

10g (⅓oz) red modelling paste
   (see page 68)

Candy stick

Four strawberry liquorice sticks

Tiny amount of black sugarpaste

Tools:

27mm (1⅛in) heart cutter

Small drinking straw

Non-stick rolling pin

Thin palette knife

Plastic sandwich bag

Water brush

Dresden tool or cocktail stick

Scrunched-up paper tissue

Instructions:

1 For the wings, roll out the red modelling paste and cut out two hearts with the heart cutter. Roll a cocktail stick over the rounded edges to frill them slightly. Leave to dry for a few hours or overnight.

2 For the legs, cut two strawberry liquorice sticks to 6.5cm (2½in), and cut them to a point for the feet. For the shoes, shape two pea-sized pieces of red sugarpaste to a point. Dampen the pointed ends of the legs and attach the shoes to them.

3 For the arms, cut two strawberry liquorice sticks to 5cm (2in), and cut them to an angle for the shoulder ends. For the hands, make two pea-sized pieces of red sugarpaste to form simple hand shapes, cut out a tiny triangle from each to form thumbs. Dampen the flat ends of the arms and attach the hands.

4 Make an egg shape of the red sugarpaste for the body with a candy stick for support, slightly sticking out. Dampen the top ends of the legs and push into the body.

5 Make petals for the skirt as in step 5 on page 71 and attach them around the body.

6 Dampen the top ends of the arms and push them into the body.

7 Make the head as on pages 70–71.

8 Make and attach red hair as in step 7, page 71. Dampen the end of the candy stick neck, and attach the head.

9 To make the rose hat, form one pea-sized piece of red modelling paste to a small sausage shape. Flatten along one edge and roll it up along the thicker edge to form a spiral. Make nine more pea-sized pieces of red modelling paste. Flatten them by pressing around the edge in a plastic sandwich bag. Attach three petals, overlapping and dampening if necessary. Stick on another two or three petals, then attach them to the top of the head, finishing off with the remaining petals. Make more petals if necessary.

10 Attach the wings with thick edible glue (see page 69). Prop them up with scrunched-up paper tissue until the glue is dry.

Go Green!

As an alternative, you can use green liquorice sticks for the arms and legs and white sugarpaste for the rest of the fairy. These two make a beautiful, petal-covered pair.

Stardust Fairy

Instructions:

1 For the wings and headdress, roll out the white modelling paste and cut three stars with the medium star cutter. Dampen the surfaces of the stars and sprinkle them with edible glitter. Leave to dry for a few hours or overnight.

2 For the legs, cut two liquorice sticks to 6.5cm (2½in), and cut them to a point for the feet. For the shoes, make two pea-sized pieces of white sugarpaste and shape each one to a point. Dampen the pointed ends of the legs and attach the shoes.

3 Roll out white sugarpaste and cut out a large star for the skirt.

4 Make an egg shape of the black sugarpaste for the body with a candy stick for support, slightly sticking out. Attach the star skirt to the bottom of the body. Dampen the underside of the skirt and position the body on top of the legs.

5 For the arms, cut two liquorice sticks to 5cm (2in), and cut each one to an angle for the shoulder end. For the hands, make two pea-sized pieces of white sugarpaste to form simple hand shapes, and cut out tiny triangles

to form thumbs. Dampen the flat ends of the arms and attach the hands. Dampen the top ends of the arms and push into the body.

6 Make the head as described on pages 70–71.

7 For the hat, roll out black sugarpaste and cut out a large star. Dampen and stick to the head with the points towards the face.

8 Roll out white sugarpaste thinly. Cut out small stars and attach to the chest and knees. Cut out tiny stars and attach to the head and shoes.

9 Attach the wings and star headdress with thick edible glue (see page 69).

Materials:

10g (⅓oz) white sugarpaste

Black sugarpaste: 10g (⅓oz) for the body, 5g (⅙oz) for the hat and a tiny amount for the eyes

10g (⅓oz) white modelling paste (see page 68)

Candy stick

Four liquorice sticks

Edible glitter

Thick edible glue

Tools:

Star cutters: large, medium, small and tiny

Small drinking straw

Non-stick rolling pin

Thin palette knife

Plastic sandwich bag

Water brush

Dresden tool or cocktail stick

Scrunched up paper tissue

Starman

You can buy edible glitter in all kinds of different shades to give the stars a colourful shimmer.

Daisy Fairy

Instructions:

1 Roll out the white modelling paste and cut out a pair of butterfly wings with a large butterfly cutter. Gently brush green powder food colour over the surface. Leave to dry for a few hours or overnight.

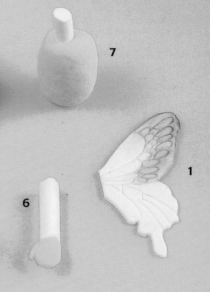

Materials:
- 20g (²⁄₃oz) green modelling paste (see page 68)
- 5g (¹⁄₆oz) flesh-coloured sugarpaste
- 5g (¹⁄₆oz) yellow modelling paste
- 5g (¹⁄₆oz) yellow sugarpaste
- 10g (¹⁄₃oz) white modelling paste
- Five candy sticks

Tiny amount of black sugarpaste
Edible powder food colour: green
Thick edible glue

Tools:
Large butterfly cutter
Dusting brush
Daisy flower cutter

Non-stick rolling pin
Small drinking straw
Thin palette knife
Plastic sandwich bag
Water brush
Dresden tool or cocktail stick
Scrunched up paper tissue

2 For the base, shape the green modelling paste to a drum shape.

3 For the shoes, make two small pea-sized pieces of yellow sugarpaste and shape each to an oval. Attach to the top of the drum.

4 For the legs, push two candy sticks straight down through one end of the shoes to the very bottom of the base. This will help support the standing figure. Attach a pea-sized piece of yellow sugarpaste on top of the legs to form the base of the body.

5 Roll out white modelling paste thinly. Cut out two daisy flowers, dampen the centres and stick them one on top of the other on the base of the body to make the skirt.

6 For the arms, cut or break two candy sticks to slightly shorter than the legs. For the hands, make two pea-sized pieces of yellow sugarpaste to form simple hand shapes and cut out a tiny triangle from each to form thumbs. Dampen the ends of the arms and attach the hands.

7 Make an egg shape of yellow modelling paste for the body with a candy stick for support, slightly sticking out for the neck. Dampen the top ends of the arms and push them into the body. Cut out two more daisy flowers and stick them on to form a collar. Attach the body to the top of the legs. Leave to dry overnight, propped upright.

8 Make the head as detailed on pages 70–71.

9 Cut out four more daisy flowers. Cut each flower into segments and stick to the head around the face. Petals can be dried close to the head (main picture, right) or opening out (detail picture, left).

10 Form a ball of yellow sugarpaste, just bigger than a pea. Flatten around the edge, widening it enough to cover the back of the head. Attach it. Texture the surface with a cocktail stick.

11 Attach the wings as detailed on page 71.

12 Use thick edible glue to stick the head on to the top of the neck.

Daisy Do

Vibrant greens and yellows give this flower fairy a wonderfully summery feel. You could make a Michaelmas Daisy fairy with purple petals.

Christmas Fairy

Instructions:

1 For the wings, press the white modelling paste into the bird wing mould. Remove from the mould and brush with edible pearl white powder. Leave to dry overnight.

2 Make a red sausage, and a white sausage of sugarpaste, each the size and length wanted for legs. Cut each leg into small segments and put these in a plastic bag to keep them soft. Stick red and white segments together alternately and form two stripey legs. Roll very gently to get the segments attached smoothly (only dampen slightly if the pieces refuse to stick). Stick the tops of the legs together, side by side.

3 For the shoes, make two pea-sized pieces of green sugarpaste and shape each one to a point. Dampen the ends of the legs and attach the shoes.

4 For the skirt, roll out red sugarpaste and cut out a circle using the circle cutter. Frill over the edge with a cocktail stick. Roll out white sugarpaste and cut out a carnation. Frill around the edge as before. Dampen under the two skirt layers and stick them on top of the legs.

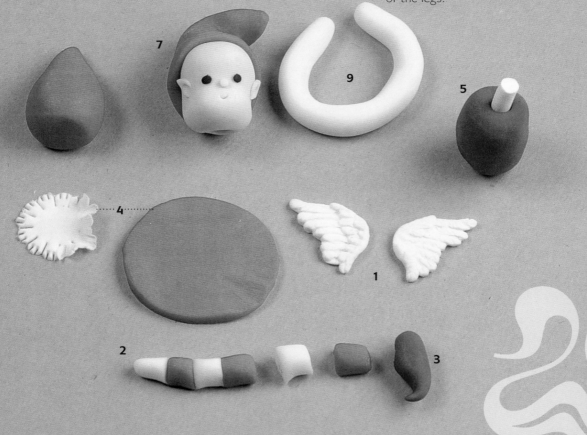

5 Take an egg shape of green sugarpaste for the body with a candy stick for support, slightly sticking out. Dampen the bottom of the body and stick it on top of the skirt.

6 Divide the rest of the green sugarpaste and form two carrot shapes for the arms. Bend to form the elbows and flatten the hands. Attach to the body.

7 Make the head as on pages 70–71. Make a cone shape from red sugarpaste for the hat. Hollow the fat end by pressing with your finger and thumb until it fits over the back of the head. Dampen the inside and attach to the head. Bend the point of the hat over to one side.

8 Dampen the end of the candy stick neck and attach the head.

9 Roll a long sausage of white sugarpaste and attach round the edge of the hat.

10 Attach the wings as on page 71.

11 To make pompoms, push a little white sugarpaste through a sieve, sugarcraft gun or garlic press. Dampen the end of the hat and the centre of the chest and then attach the pompoms.

Christmas Sweetie

This cute fairy is perfect for the Christmas table with her gift of a yellow sweet. If you just want her to be a winter fairy, make her in white sugarpaste, rather than red, white and green.

Materials:

10g (⅓oz) flesh-coloured sugarpaste

Green sugarpaste: 10g (⅓oz) for the body and 10g (⅓oz) for the arms and feet

Red sugarpaste: 10g (⅓oz) for the skirt and legs and 10g (⅓oz) for the hat

10g (⅓oz) white sugarpaste for the legs, skirt, fluff and hat

10g (⅓oz) modelling paste (see page 68)

Candy stick

Tiny amount of black sugarpaste

Edible powder food colour: pearl white

Tools:

Multi-mould for bird wings

56mm (2¼in) circle cutter

Carnation cutter

Sieve, sugarcraft gun or garlic press

Non-stick rolling pin

Small drinking straw

Thin palette knife

Plastic sandwich bag

Dusting brush

Water brush

Dresden tool or cocktail stick

Scrunched up paper tissue

Daffodil Fairy

Materials:

10g (⅓oz) flesh-coloured sugarpaste

10g (⅓oz) orange sugarpaste

10g (⅓oz) yellow sugarpaste

10g (⅓oz) orange modelling paste (see page 68) for the wings

Candy stick

Four green liquorice sticks

Tiny amount of black sugarpaste

Tools:

Carnation cutter

Large calyx (five-pointed flower) cutter

Tiny six-petal cutter

Small drinking straw

Non-stick rolling pin

Thin palette knife

Plastic sandwich bag

Water brush

Dresden tool or cocktail stick

Scrunched-up paper tissue

Instructions:

1 For the legs, cut two green liquorice sticks to 6.5cm (2½in) and cut them to points for the feet. For the shoes, make two pea-sized pieces of orange sugarpaste and shape each one to a point. Dampen the pointed ends of the legs and attach the shoes. Attach the tops of the legs to a slightly larger than pea-sized piece of sugarpaste.

2 Roll out yellow sugarpaste and cut out a large calyx for the skirt. Lay the skirt over the tops of the legs. Cut out two tiny six-petal flowers and stick them on to the shoes. Make two tiny balls of orange sugarpaste. Stick them on top of the flowers on the shoes and make a tiny hole in the middle of each ball.

3 Make an egg shape of the orange sugarpaste for the body with a candy stick for support, slightly sticking out. Mark a few lines with a knife on the orange paste. Dampen the bottom of the body and position it on top of the legs.

4 For the arms, cut two green liquorice sticks to 5cm (2in) and cut each one to an angle for the shoulder end. For the hands, make two pea-sized pieces of orange sugarpaste and shape each one into a simple hand, then cut out tiny triangles to form thumbs. Dampen the flat ends of the arms and attach the hands. Dampen the top ends of the arms and push them into the body.

5 Roll out orange modelling paste thinly. Cut out two carnation flowers. Frill around the edge with a cocktail stick. Attach one over the neck for a collar. Cut the second one in half and stick the straight edges along the backs of the arms to make the wings.

6 Make the head as described on pages 70–71.

7 For the hair, make lots of small carrot-shaped pieces of yellow sugarpaste. Dampen the head and attach the strands of hair with the pointed ends towards the face and neck. When the head is covered with enough strands of hair, dampen the end of the candy stick neck and attach the head.

8 Cut out and frill another orange carnation flower and attach to the back of the head.

Cloud Host

This bright and breezy fairy would be perfect for someone with a spring birthday, or for St David's Day.

Little Princess Fairy

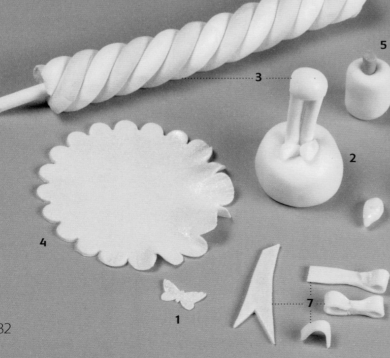

Materials:

White modelling paste (see page 68): 20g (⅔oz) for the base and 5g (⅙oz) for the body

10g (⅓oz) modelling paste

5g (⅙oz) flesh-coloured sugarpaste

5g (⅙oz) yellow sugarpaste

Three candy sticks

Tiny amount of black sugarpaste

Edible powder food colour: pearl white

Edible glitter

Thick edible glue

Tools:

Small butterfly cutter

Multi-mould for the crown

Garrett frill cutter (large fluted round cutter)

Dusting brush

Non-stick rolling pin

Small drinking straw

Thin palette knife

Plastic sandwich bag

Dresden tool or cocktail stick

Scrunched up paper tissue

Water brush

Instructions:

1 For the wings, roll out the white modelling paste and cut out two butterflies with the small cutter. Gently brush pearl white powder food colour over the surface. Leave to dry for a few hours or overnight.

2 For the base, shape the white modelling paste to a drum shape.

3 For the shoes, make two pea-sized pieces of white sugarpaste and shape each to a point. Attach to the top of the drum. For the legs, push two candy sticks straight down through one end of the shoes to the very bottom of the drum. This will help to support the standing figure. Attach a pea-sized piece of white sugarpaste on top of the legs to form the base of the body. To decorate the stand I used a length of twirly marshmallow, pushed a candy stick in one end then wrapped the marshmallow around the base.

The other end of the candy stick was then pushed into the end of the marshmallow to secure it, at the back of the base.

4 Roll out white modelling paste thinly. Cut out one garrett frill. Frill around the edge with a cocktail stick. Dampen the centre and stick on top of the base of the body to make the skirt. Stick the skirt on top of the legs, making it shorter at the front and longer at the back.

5 Make an egg shape of white modelling paste for the body with a candy stick for support, slightly sticking out for the neck. Dampen it and attach it on top on the legs and skirt. Leave to dry overnight.

6 Cut out a thin strip of rolled-out white modelling paste to make the ribbon waistband. Dust with pearl white powder. Dampen around the waist and attach the ribbon. Join at the back and cut off the excess.

7 For the bow, cut two ribbon tails from sugarpaste, dust with pearl white and attach at the join of the waistband. Cut out a short ribbon, twice the length of the desired bow. Dust, as before. Dampen the middle point of the ribbon and bring both ends into the middle to stick. Stick on to the top of the ribbon tails. Finish with a short piece of dusted ribbon across the middle of the bow.

8 Divide 5g (1/6oz) of the sugarpaste and form two carrot shapes for the arms. Bend to form the elbows and flatten the hands. Attach to the body.

9 Attach the wings as described on page 71. Attach the other butterfly to the hands.

10 Make the head as described on pages 70–71.

11 For the hair, make short carrots of yellow sugarpaste. Attach to the head, shaping into a style and marking strands with a Dresden tool.

12 Make a crown in the mould. Dampen it and sprinkle it with edible glitter. Attach it to the top of the head.

13 Use thick edible glue to stick the head on top of the neck.

Fairytale

This sweet fairy is sure to delight the little princess in your life!

Bathing Fairy

Instructions:

1 For the wings, roll out the white modelling paste and cut with a large butterfly cutter. Gently brush blue powder food colour over the surface. Leave to dry for a few hours or overnight.

2 Make an egg shape of flesh-coloured sugarpaste for the body with a candy stick for support, slightly sticking out. Make a dip in the sugarpaste in the teacup, dampen it and attach the body,

leaning against the inside of the teacup. Make sure the tops of the shoulders are above the rim of the cup.

3 Make the head as described on pages 70–71.

Materials:

- Flesh-coloured sugarpaste: 10g (⅓oz) for the head, 10g (⅓oz) for the body and 10g (⅓oz) for the arms
- 10g (⅓oz) modelling paste (see page 68)
- 10g (⅓oz) blue sugarpaste
- Tiny amount of black sugarpaste
- Pretty teacup filled with sugarpaste
- Edible blue powder colour
- Extra white sugarpaste
- Candy stick

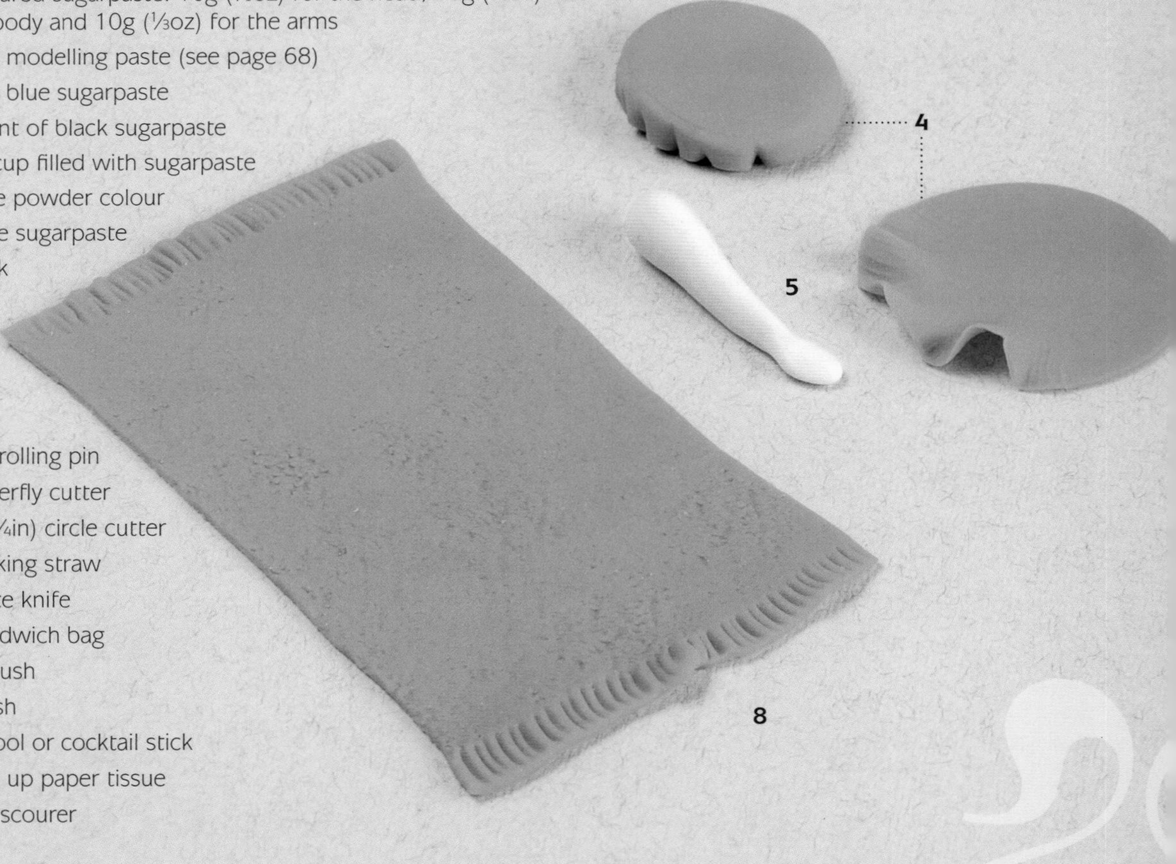

Tools:

- Non-stick rolling pin
- Large butterfly cutter
- 56mm (2¼in) circle cutter
- Small drinking straw
- Thin palette knife
- Plastic sandwich bag
- Dusting brush
- Water brush
- Dresden tool or cocktail stick
- Scrunched up paper tissue
- Clean pan scourer

4

5

8

4 Roll out blue sugarpaste for the hat. Cut out two of the circles. Frill one circle and attach to the top of the head. Turn the edges of the other circle under to look gathered and attach to the top of the frilled circle.

5 Divide the rest of the flesh-coloured sugarpaste and form two carrot shapes for the arms. Bend to form the elbows and flatten the hands. Attach to the body.

6 Attach the wings as on page 71.

7 Make lots of pea-sized pieces of white sugarpaste, and dust with edible pearl colour, top up the bath with these bubbles and sprinkle with edible glitter.

8 If you want to make a bath mat or towel, roll out blue sugarpaste, texture it with a clean scourer and mark a fringe on each end by pressing lines with a Dresden tool or cocktail stick.

Bath Night

Have fun looking for pretty teacups or bowls for this fairy to use for her bath. She would make a great gift for someone who likes a good soak.

Sunshine Fairy

Instructions:

1 Make an egg shape of yellow sugarpaste for the body with a candy stick for support, slightly sticking out. Lay the body on its back.

2 For the legs, divide the piece of paste in two. Roll each piece to a long carrot shape about twice the length of the body. Bend in the middle for the knee, and bend to form the foot. Attach the legs to the body, with knees up and feet on the surface.

3 For the wings, roll out yellow sugarpaste and cut out one large flower. Cut it in half and attach under the body.

4 Cut out at least four large flowers, cut them in quarters and attach to the body to form the skirt.

5 For the arms, divide the piece of sugarpaste and form two carrot shapes, slightly longer than the body. Bend to form the elbows, and flatten the hands. Attach to the body.

6 Make the head as on pages 70–71. Instead of making eyes, make two larger circles of black, cut the top edge off, stick on and draw the frames for the sunglasses with the food colour felt-tip pen.

7 For the hair, cut out two more large yellow flowers and stick one over the head, and the second one lying flat under the head. Dampen the end of the candy stick neck and attach the head.

Materials:

10g (⅓oz) flesh-coloured sugarpaste

Yellow sugarpaste: 10g (⅓oz) for the body, 10g (⅓oz) for the legs, 5g (⅙oz) for the arms and 10g (⅓oz) for the skirt, hat and wings

Candy stick

Small amount of black sugarpaste

Tools:

Large eight-petal flower cutter

Food colour felt-tip pen

Non-stick rolling pin

Small drinking straw

Thin palette knife

Plastic sandwich bag

Water brush

Dresden tool or cocktail stick

Sunbeam

This brilliant fairy just loves to stretch out and catch some rays. You could make her for a sun worshipper you know.

Tooth Fairy

Instructions:

1 For the wings, cut the leaf gelatine with scissors to a simple butterfly shape. Carefully paint the edge with egg white and sprinkle with edible glitter. Shake off the excess and leave to dry for a few hours or overnight.

2 Make the legs from two candy sticks. For the shoes, make two pea-sized pieces of purple sugarpaste and shape each one to a point. Attach the shoes.

3 For the body, make an egg shape of purple sugarpaste with a candy stick for support, sticking out a little. Push the top ends of the legs into the body.

4 Roll out white sugarpaste. Cut out at least seven heart shapes, and attach on to the body for the skirt.

5 Make a sugar toothbrush using a candy stick. Shape a slightly larger than pea-sized piece of white sugarpaste to a solid block shape. Attach to the end of the sugar stick, and mark bristles using a knife.

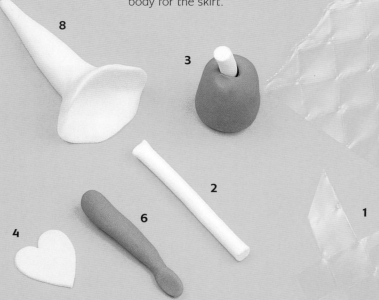

Pearly Queen

Have you ever wondered who was leaving coins under your pillow? Well here she is, a fairy with a sweet tooth but also a toothbrush to keep her teeth sparkling white and clean!

6 Divide the piece of purple sugarpaste for the arms and form two carrot shapes, slightly longer than the body. Bend to form the elbows, and flatten the hands. Attach to the body, and stick one hand to the toothbrush.

7 Make the head as described on pages 70–71.

8 For the hat, use white sugarpaste the same size as the head. Shape to a long cone. Flatten the wide end between your finger and thumb until it is big enough to cover the back of the head. Shape the pointed end to a spiral, to look like toothpaste. Attach the head to the body.

9 Roll out white sugarpaste and cut out lots of small stars, one for each shoe and the rest all around the edge between the hat and the head, overlapping.

10 Attach the wings as on page 71.

Materials:
10g (⅓oz) flesh-coloured sugarpaste
Purple sugarpaste: 10g (⅓oz) for the body and 10g (⅓oz) for the shoes and arms
10g (⅓oz) white sugarpaste
Tiny amount of black sugarpaste
Leaf gelatine for the wings
Six candy sticks
Edible glitter
Egg white

Tools:
18mm (¾in) heart cutter
Small star cutter
Scissors
Non-stick rolling pin
Small drinking straw
Thin palette knife
Plastic sandwich bag
Water brush
Dresden tool or cocktail stick
Scrunched up paper tissue

Fairy Godmother

Materials:

Pink modelling paste
   (see page 68): 35g (1¼oz) for
   the body, 10g (⅓oz) for the arms
   and cape

5g (⅙oz) flesh-coloured
   sugarpaste

5g (⅙oz) white sugarpaste

Candy stick

Edible powder food colour:
   pearl white

Egg white

Tools:

Garrett frill cutter (large fluted
   round cutter)

Large butterfly cutter

Tiny star cutter

Scissors

Dusting brush

Non-stick rolling pin

Small drinking straw

Thin palette knife

Plastic sandwich bag

Water brush

Dresden tool or cocktail stick

Instructions:

1 For the wings, roll out the
white modelling paste and cut out
a large butterfly and a tiny star.
Gently brush pearl white powder
food colour over the surfaces.
Frill over the edge of the butterfly
using a Dresden tool or cocktail
stick. Leave to dry for a few hours.

2 For the body, make a pear
shape from pink modelling paste
with a candy stick for support,
slightly sticking out for the neck.

3 For the cape, roll out pink
modelling paste thinly. Cut out one
garrett frill. Dampen the back of
the body. Wrap the cape around

the body, slightly higher at the shoulders as shown.

4 Divide 5g (⅙oz) of the pink modelling paste and form two carrot shapes for the arms. Bend to form the elbows, and flatten the hands. Attach to the body.

5 Attach the wings as on page 71, and the star on one hand.

6 Make the head as described on pages 70–71.

7 For the hair, make small carrots of white sugarpaste. Attach to the head, shaping into a style.

Mark extra strands of hair with a Dresden tool or cocktail stick. Attach a pea-sized piece to form a bun on top.

8 Use thick edible glue to stick the head on top of the neck.

Wanda

This beautiful fairy godmother looks as though she could fix anything for you! She would make a lovely gift for a godmother or just a friend who has helped you out.

Fairy Bride

Materials:

- White modelling paste (see page 68): 35g (1¼oz) for the body and 10g (⅓oz) for the arms and skirt
- 5g (⅙oz) flesh-coloured sugarpaste
- 5g (⅙oz) white sugarpaste
- 5g (⅙oz) pink modelling paste for the flowers
- 5g (⅙oz) green modelling paste for the flowers
- Candy stick
- Edible wafer paper or rice paper
- Edible powder food colour: pearl white
- Edible glitter
- Egg white
- Thick edible glue

Tools:

- Garrett frill cutter (large fluted round cutter)
- Tiny blossom cutter
- Scissors
- Food colour felt-tip pen
- Dusting brush
- Non-stick rolling pin
- Small drinking straw
- Thin palette knife
- Plastic sandwich bag
- Water brush
- Dresden tool
- Cocktail stick

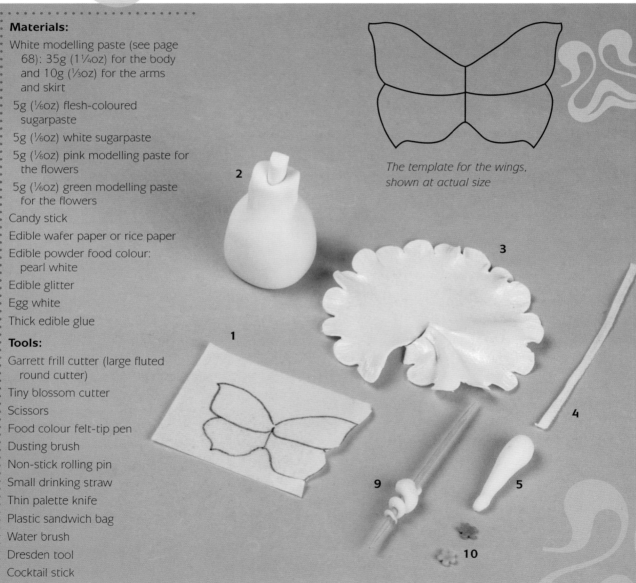

The template for the wings, shown at actual size

Instructions:

1 For the wings, trace the butterfly template (left) on to edible wafer paper or rice paper and cut out the shape. Carefully paint egg white around the edge and sprinkle with edible glitter. Shake off the excess. Leave to dry for a few hours or overnight.

2 For the body, make a pear shape from white modelling paste with a candy stick for support, slightly sticking out for the neck.

3 Roll out white modelling paste thinly. Cut out one garrett frill. Dust all over with edible pearl white powder. Frill around the edge with a cocktail stick. Cut a line straight from the edge to the middle. Dampen the waist on the body. Attach the skirt, gathering the waist along the cut edges as necessary.

4 Cut out a thin strip of rolled-out white modelling paste to make the ribbon for the waistband. Dust with pearl white powder. Dampen around the waist and attach the ribbon. Join at the back and cut off any excess.

5 Divide 5g (⅙oz) of white sugarpaste and form two carrot shapes for the arms. Bend to form the elbows and flatten the hands. Attach to the body. Attach a small pea-sized piece of pink sugarpaste to the fairy's hands for the bouquet.

6 Attach the wings, using egg white as glue.

7 Make the head as on pages 70–71, but use the drinking straw to mark the closed eyes.

8 Use thick edible glue to stick the head on top of the neck.

9 For the hair, make long strands of white sugarpaste. Attach to the head, shaping into a style. Twirl some of the strands around a cocktail stick to make ringlets before attaching them.

10 Thinly roll out the pink and green sugarpaste. Cut out tiny green blossoms and attach them to the top of the head to form a headdress, and over the base of the bouquet. Then cut out tiny pink blossoms and attach them over the green ones, hiding the green as much as possible.

Fairytale Wedding
This blushing bride would be perfect for a fairy lover's wedding cake.

Cuddly Fairy

Materials:

Flesh-coloured sugarpaste: 10g (⅓oz) for the head, 20g (⅔oz) for the body, 20g (⅔oz) for the legs and 10g (⅓oz) for the arms

10g (⅓oz) pink sugarpaste

5g (⅙oz) dark pink sugarpaste

5g (⅙oz) white sugarpaste

5g (⅙oz) brown sugarpaste or modelling chocolate

Candy stick

Tiny amount of black sugarpaste for the eyes

Edible wafer paper or rice paper

Egg white

Edible glitter

Tools:

27mm (1in) heart cutter

Circle cutters: 56mm (2¼in), 41mm (1⅝in)

Small blossom cutter

Scissors

Food colour felt-tip pen

Non-stick rolling pin

Small drinking straw

Thin palette knife

Plastic sandwich bag

Water brush

Dresden tool or cocktail stick

Instructions:

1 For the wings, trace the butterfly wings from page 92 on to edible wafer paper or rice paper and cut them out. Carefully paint egg white around the edge and sprinkle with edible glitter. Shake off the excess. Leave to dry for a few hours.

2 For the body, make an upside-down pear shape of flesh-coloured sugarpaste with a candy stick for support, slightly sticking out.

3 Divide the piece of paste for the legs. Roll each piece to a long carrot shape, about twice the length of the body. Attach small cones in dark pink sugarpaste for the shoes. Stick the legs together.

4 Roll out white sugarpaste thinly. Cut out at least two of the smaller circles. Frill around the edge with a cocktail stick. Dampen the middle of each and attach over the top of the legs. Repeat, using the pink sugarpaste and the larger circles. Dampen the bottom of the body and attach to middle of the skirt.

5 Attach a pink sugarpaste heart for the front of the dress, and small blossoms around the waist.

6 For the arms, divide the piece of flesh-coloured sugarpaste and form two carrot shapes, slightly longer than the body. Bend to form the elbows, and flatten the hands. Attach to the body.

7 Make the head as described on pages 70–71.

8 For the hair, make lots of small carrot-shaped pieces of brown sugarpaste. Dampen the head and attach the strands of hair with the pointed ends towards the face and neck. When the head is covered,

attach a circlet of white blossoms for the headdress.

9 Dampen the end of the candy stick neck, and attach the head.

10 Attach the wings using egg white as glue.

Bumbleina

Just to prove that fairies are not all tiny and ethereal, here's a big, buxom and beautiful fairy who is sweetness itself.

Publishers' Note
If you would like more books about sugarcraft, try
Sensational Sugar Animals by Frances McNaughton, Search Press 2012; and
Cupcakes & Cookies by Frances McNaughton and Lisa Slatter, Search Press 2009.

You are invited to visit the author's website:
franklysweet.co.uk